inside
CARS,
trucks & bikes

inside
CARS, trucks & bikes

By Steve Parker
Illustrated by Alex Pang

Miles Kelly

First published in 2009 by Miles Kelly Publishing Ltd
Harding's Barn, Bardfield End Green, Thaxted, Essex, CM6 3PX, UK

Copyright © Miles Kelly Publishing Ltd 2009

This edition printed in 2012

10 9 8 7 6 5 4 3 2 1

Publishing Director: *Belinda Gallagher*
Creative Director: *Jo Cowan*
Design Concept: *Simon Lee*
Volume Design: *Rocket Design*
Cover Designer: *Simon Lee*
Indexer: *Gill Lee*
Production Manager: *Elizabeth Collins*
Reprographics: *Stephan Davis, Thom Allaway*
Consultants: *John and Sue Becklake*
Edition Editor: *Amanda Askew*

ISBN 978-1-84810-830-1

629.2

Printed in China

British Library Cataloguing-in-Publication Data
A catalogue record for this book is available from the British Library

MADE WITH PAPER FROM
A SUSTAINABLE FOREST

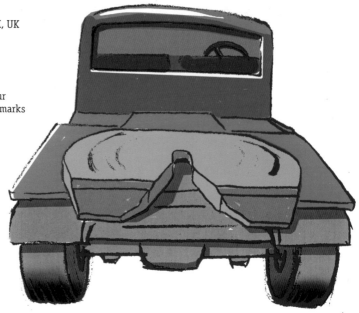

ACKNOWLEDGEMENTS

All panel artworks by Rocket Design
The publishers would like to thank the following
sources for the use of their photographs:
Alamy: 29 Motoring Picture Library
Corbis: 25 Transtock; 35 Thinkstock
Fotolia: 15 Sculpies
Getty Images: 33 James Balog
Rex Features: 7(c) The Travel Library; 13 KPA/Zama
Science Photo Library: 6(t) LIBRARY OF CONGRESS;
All other photographs are from Miles Kelly Archives
Shutterstock: COVER digitalsport-photoagency,
Herbert Kratky; 7(b) Natursports; 9 Chad McDermott;
11 Herbert Kratky; 17; 19 Max Earey; 21 Chen Wei Seng;
23 Manfred Steinbach; 26 Walter G Arce;
30 Chris Jenner; 36 Mike Brake

WWW.FACTSFORPROJECTS.COM

Each top right-hand page directs
you to the Internet to help you
find out more. You can log on
to **www.factsforprojects.com**
to find free pictures, additional
information, videos, fun activities
and further web links. These
are for your own personal use
and should not be copied or
distributed for any commercial
or profit-related purpose.

If you do decide to use the
Internet with your book, here's a
list of what you'll need:
• A PC with Microsoft® Windows®
  XP or later versions, or a
  Macintosh with OS X or later,
  and 512Mb RAM

• A browser such as Microsoft®
  Internet Explorer 9, Firefox 4.X
  or Safari 5.X
• Connection to the Internet.
  Broadband connection
  recommended.
• An account with an Internet
  Service Provider (ISP)
• A sound card for listening to
  sound files

Links won't work?
www.factsforprojects.com is
regularly checked to make sure
the links provide you with lots
of information. Sometimes you
may receive a message saying
that a site is unavailable. If this
happens, just try again later.

Stay safe!
When using the Internet, make
sure you follow these guidelines:
• Ask a parent's or a guardian's
  permission before you log on.
• Never give out your personal
  details, such as your name,
  address or email.
• If a site asks you to log in or
  register by typing your name
  or email address, speak to your
  parent or guardian first.
• If you do receive an email from
  someone you don't know, tell
  an adult and do not reply to the
  message.
• Never arrange to meet anyone
  you have talked to on the
  Internet.

Miles Kelly Publishing is not
responsible for the accuracy or
suitability of the information on
any website other than its own.
We recommend that children are
supervised while on the Internet
and that they do not use Internet
chat rooms.

www.mileskelly.net
info@mileskelly.net

CONTENTS

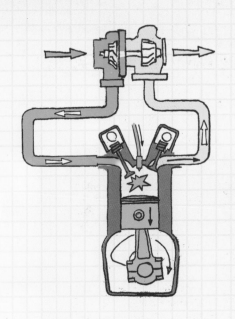

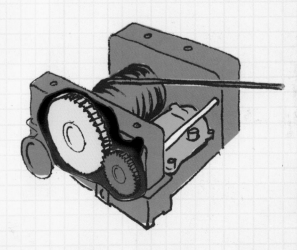

INTRODUCTION

The wheel was invented about 6000 years ago in western Asia. Initially it was a potter's wheel, used for shaping clay bowls and vases. By 3500 years ago, wheels were in use on wagons and chariots pulled by horses, oxen or slaves. It took another 3300 years to invent wheeled vehicles with engines. Just before them, the first bicycles appeared. They had no pedals – you pushed your feet against the ground. Then came personal engine-driven transport, and we have never looked back – except to see who is behind.

The penny-farthing bicycle of the 1870s had direct drive, with pedals attached to the wheel.

Bicycle gears make pedalling easier or faster, but not both.

In 'green gear' the green-driven sprocket turns twice

Frame

Red-driven sprocket turns once

Pedal

In 'orange gear' the smaller orange-driven sprocket turns three times

Chain can be switched between 'driven' sprockets, which are attached to the rear wheel

ON THE ROAD

The first pedal-powered bicycles and engine-driven cars and motorcycles appeared towards the end of the 1800s. Most transport was still animal-drawn and roads were little more than dirt tracks with sharp stones and deep holes. Many early cars were steam- or electric-powered, and most were hand-built in the tradition of horse-drawn carriages.

MOTORING FOR ALL

In 1908 the American Ford Motor Company introduced an assembly line where lots of identical cars could be put together from already-made parts. Suddenly, vehicles were cheaper and demand grew. By the 1950s some cars were huge, covered with shiny chrome and lined with leather. Real mass motoring took hold in the 1960s with smaller 'budget' cars such as the VW Beetle and the Mini.

The British Mini was not only a very small car but also a fashion item and symbol of the 1960s.

The vehicles featured in this book are Internet linked.
Visit www.factsforprojects.com to find out more.

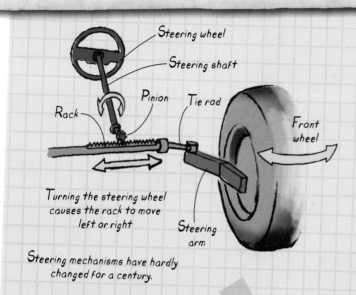

Steering wheel

Steering shaft

Pinion

Tie rod

Rack

Front wheel

Turning the steering wheel causes the rack to move left or right

Steering arm

Steering mechanisms have hardly changed for a century.

BRANCHING OUT

As road vehicles became more powerful and more reliable, they evolved into new kinds. Today there are huge lorries to transport loads, emergency vehicles such as fire appliances and breakdown services, all-wheel-drive off-roaders and pick-ups to carry almost anything. More gears, better brakes, stronger engines and smoother suspension help to make these vehicles more efficient and the ride more comfortable. Whether dashing to the shops in the family car, messing about on bicycles, boarding the school bus or cruising the empty freeway, road vehicles are vital in our daily lives.

Massive road trains are used to transport goods across the vast open areas of Australia.

THE RACE IS ON!

Any new way of going places meant that people wanted to be there first. Cycling races and motor sports blossomed, from rallying to track events to dragster duels. In today's Formula One, super-fast cars that cost tens of millions race in front of the biggest audiences on the planet.

Motor vehicles have come a long way in a century, but with fossil fuels running out and global warming on the increase, could we live without them?

More than 600 million TV viewers watch each Formula One race.

MOUNTAIN BIKE

The overall design of the bicycle has hardly changed for more than 100 years. It is made up of many simple machines or basic mechanical devices such as levers, wheels and axles, pulleys, gears and springs. A bicycle also gives its rider exercise to stay healthy, and because it has no engine and polluting exhaust gases, it's excellent for the environment.

Mountain-biking became an official Olympic sport in 1996 – 100 years after ordinary cycle racing.

Eureka!

The first bicycles were developed in Germany and France during the 1810s. However they had no pedals. Riders had to push the ground with their feet to 'scoot' along.

Whatever next?

Electric bicycles are predicted to become much more popular, complete with a see-through, bubble-like cover to keep you dry.

Gear changer A device called the derailleur moves the chain sideways from one sprocket to another, to change gear.

Spring suspension When the rear wheel goes over a bump, its frame tilts up and squeezes a large spring to absorb the shock.

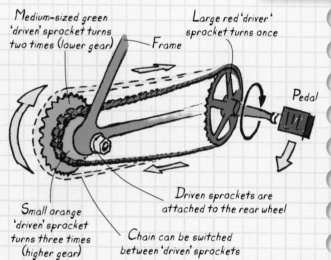

Medium-sized green 'driven' sprocket turns two times (lower gear)

Large red 'driver' sprocket turns once

Frame

Pedal

Driven sprockets are attached to the rear wheel

Small orange 'driven' sprocket turns three times (higher gear)

Chain can be switched between 'driven' sprockets

✳ How do CHAIN AND SPROCKET GEARS work?

A bicycle's rear sprockets or cogs have different numbers of teeth. In a low gear, each turn of the front sprocket (attached to the pedals) means the rear sprocket (attached to the wheel) turns twice. You don't go very far for one turn of the front sprocket but pedalling is less effort. In a higher gear, the chain moves to a smaller sprocket. This turns three times for one turn of the front sprocket. So you go farther for each turn of the pedals but pedalling is more effort. The idea is to change gear to keep your pedalling speed and effort constant, at the best rate for you.

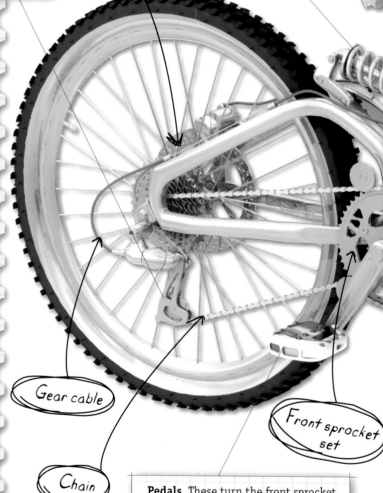

Rear sprocket set

Gear cable

Chain

Pedals These turn the front sprocket whose teeth fit into the chain link gaps. This provides a non-slip way to turn the rear sprocket.

Front sprocket set

Learn how to use bicycle gears by visiting
www.factsforprojects.com and clicking on the web link.

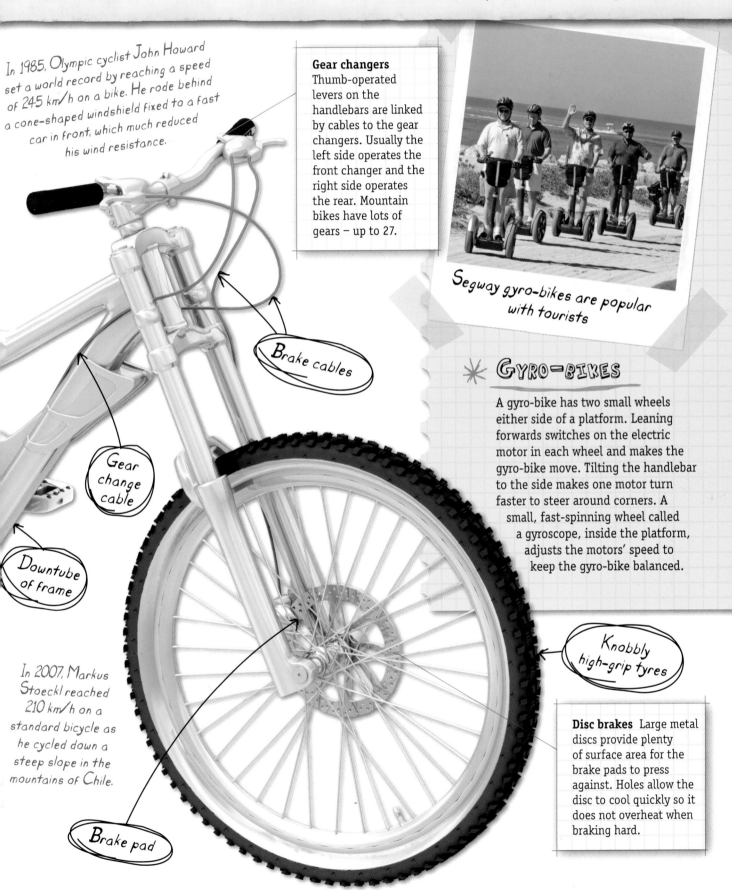

In 1985, Olympic cyclist John Howard set a world record by reaching a speed of 245 km/h on a bike. He rode behind a cone-shaped windshield fixed to a fast car in front, which much reduced his wind resistance.

Gear changers
Thumb-operated levers on the handlebars are linked by cables to the gear changers. Usually the left side operates the front changer and the right side operates the rear. Mountain bikes have lots of gears – up to 27.

Segway gyro-bikes are popular with tourists

Brake cables

* GYRO-BIKES

A gyro-bike has two small wheels either side of a platform. Leaning forwards switches on the electric motor in each wheel and makes the gyro-bike move. Tilting the handlebar to the side makes one motor turn faster to steer around corners. A small, fast-spinning wheel called a gyroscope, inside the platform, adjusts the motors' speed to keep the gyro-bike balanced.

Gear change cable

Downtube of frame

In 2007, Markus Stoeckl reached 210 km/h on a standard bicycle as he cycled down a steep slope in the mountains of Chile.

Knobbly high-grip tyres

Disc brakes Large metal discs provide plenty of surface area for the brake pads to press against. Holes allow the disc to cool quickly so it does not overheat when braking hard.

Brake pad

ROAD RACE BICYCLE

The road race bicycle is the specialist long-distance machine of the cycling world. It's much lighter than a commuter or mountain bike and is more stripped-down and simpler too, with fewer moving parts to go wrong. The best road-racers easily cover 200 kilometres in one day, even in bad weather.

Eureka!

The first bicycles had solid wood or metal wheel rims, then solid rubber tyres – not very comfortable. The pneumatic or air-filled tyre was invented in 1887 by John Boyd Dunlop for his son's bicycle.

Ball bearings A typical bicycle has up to ten sets of ball bearings. Two in the head tube support the handlebars and front forks.

Head tube

Front fork

Racing handlebars Curled-down racing, or dropped handlebars, mean the rider leans forwards, head down. This causes less air resistance than sitting upright and allows the legs to press harder on the pedals.

✳ How do BALL BEARINGS work?

A bearing reduces rubbing or friction where one part of a machine moves against another. It decreases wear and lessens the movement energy lost as heat. In a ball bearing design, hard metal balls fit snugly between outer and inner ring-shaped parts called races. The balls can rotate in all directions, which spreads out both the wear over their surfaces and any heat from friction to prevent overheating.

Outer race (ring) rotates, gliding on steel balls

Inner race (ring) is usually fixed to shaft or axle

Shaft

Chromed-steel balls roll easily in any direction

Low-profile tyres Narrow and 'low', the side wall height is less than the tyre width, which gives extra grip but a bumpy ride.

Discover everything you need to know about the world's greatest bicycle race by visiting www.factsforprojects.com and clicking on the web link.

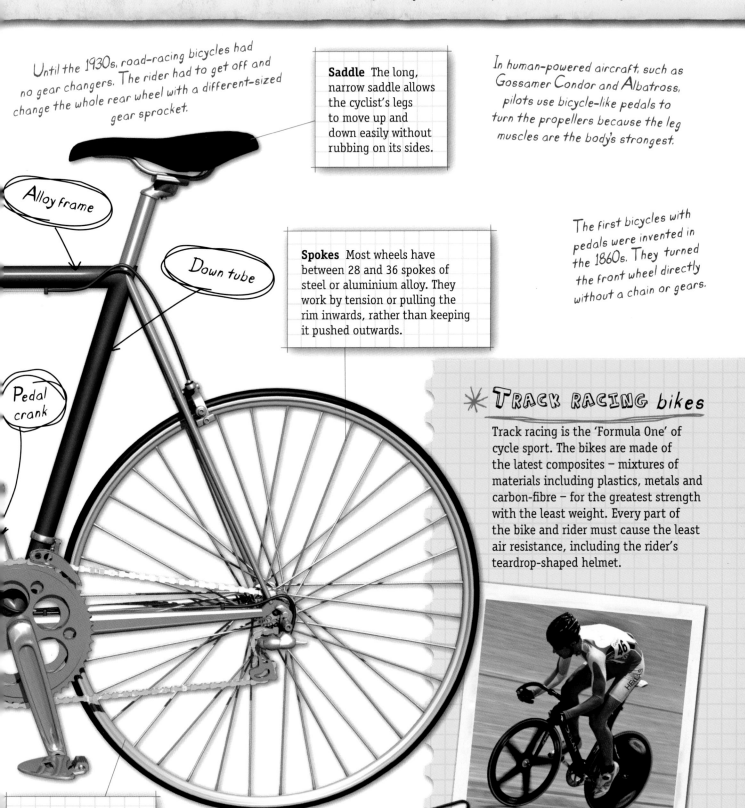

Until the 1930s, road-racing bicycles had no gear changers. The rider had to get off and change the whole rear wheel with a different-sized gear sprocket.

Saddle The long, narrow saddle allows the cyclist's legs to move up and down easily without rubbing on its sides.

In human-powered aircraft, such as *Gossamer Condor* and *Albatross*, pilots use bicycle-like pedals to turn the propellers because the leg muscles are the body's strongest.

Alloy frame

Down tube

Spokes Most wheels have between 28 and 36 spokes of steel or aluminium alloy. They work by tension or pulling the rim inwards, rather than keeping it pushed outwards.

The first bicycles with pedals were invented in the 1860s. They turned the front wheel directly without a chain or gears.

Pedal crank

✳ TRACK RACING bikes

Track racing is the 'Formula One' of cycle sport. The bikes are made of the latest composites – mixtures of materials including plastics, metals and carbon-fibre – for the greatest strength with the least weight. Every part of the bike and rider must cause the least air resistance, including the rider's teardrop-shaped helmet.

Wheel rim The rim is made of a lightweight alloy – a special combination of several kinds of metals, including aluminium.

In 1899, Charles Minthorn Murphy was first to pedal one mile (1.6 km) in less than a minute – 57.75 seconds to be exact.

Track racers keep their heads down to reduce drag

TOURING MOTORCYCLE

Long and low, the touring motorcycle is one of the coolest-looking machines on the road. It may not be the fastest on two wheels but it cruises the highways in great comfort. The bike has plenty of suspension to soak up the lumps and bumps and lots of power to overtake at speed and travel long distances.

Eureka!

In 1885 Gottlieb Daimler fitted his newly designed petrol engine into the frame of a wooden bicycle and invented the first motorcycle, the Reitwagen ('Riding Car'). Motorbikes went into mass production in 1894 with the 1500cc Hildebrand & Wolfmüller.

Whatever next?

Electric motorcycles and electric scooters become more popular and faster every year – the speed record is 270 kilometres per hour!

HARLEY DAVIDSON

'Bucket' seat

Cylinder cooling fins

Coil spring damper suspension

Exhaust pipes These long tubes mean exhaust gases are directed out of the engine so that it works more efficiently. They also reduce or muffle the engine's noise.

✳ How does COIL SPRING DAMPER suspension work?

Spring suspension absorbs holes, bumps and other rough parts of the road. However when a spring is squeezed and then allowed to push and lengthen again, it tends to 'bounce' back, shortening and lengthening several times. This is reduced by adding a hydraulic damper inside the spring. It's a tube filled with sealed-in oil, into which a smaller tube slides like a telescope. The thick oil slows down and smooths out any fast sliding movements to reduce or dampen the 'bounce' effect.

Upper mounting fixes to motorcycle frame

Oil-filled damper reduces the 'bounce' caused by the spring

Strong coil spring compresses as the vehicle goes over a bump

Lower mounting fixes to wheel's suspension arm

Transmission A series of gears transfers the engine's turning power to the drive belt and then on to the rear wheel.

Some motorcycles have a small sidecar for passengers, complete with its own wheel

Watch a video of a Harley Davidson touring motorcycle by visiting www.factsforprojects.com and clicking on the web link.

Throttle A twistgrip on the right handlebar is linked to the engine by a cable. It allows more fuel to enter the engine so it goes faster.

The world-famous Harley Davidson touring motorcycles began in 1903 when friends William Harley and Arthur Davidson produced a one-cylinder version for racing.

Fuel tank The rounded fuel tank just in front of the rider is made of very strong metal.

Forks Long front forks allow the front wheel plenty of room to move up when it hits a rough patch of road, which smooths out the ride.

Mudguard

Brake caliper

Brake disc

Engine The two-cylinder 1584cc engine is low down between the two wheels, which makes the motorcycle more stable and less likely to tip over sideways.

✳ What is a MAXI-SCOOTER?

Scooters usually have smaller wheels than motorcycles and streamlined coverings called fairings over most of the vehicle. Older scooters were not very fast or well-balanced. New maxi-scooters are faster, more comfortable, safer, change gear automatically and can be fitted with a petrol engine or electric motor.

Maxi-scooters make ideal runabouts

SUPERBIKE

Few road machines can accelerate (pick up speed) or travel as fast as the superbike – a high-powered, souped-up motorcycle. These fierce-looking machines are road versions of even faster track-racing motorcycles. Because of their great power, light weight and sensitive steering, they are tricky to ride and definitely not for the beginner.

Eureka!

Before the 1950s, riders had to kick-start their motorcycles by pushing down a pedal to turn over the engine. On most modern bikes this is done by an electric motor, as in a car.

Whatever next?

Motorcycle stunt riders are always inventing new tricks – such as speeding off a jump ramp and somersaulting two or three times.

A typical racing superbike can reach an amazing 300 km/h – but on the track, not on ordinary roads!

Clutch lever The clutch disconnects the engine from the gearbox so the rider can change gear without damaging the spinning cogs inside (see page 18).

Windscreen The clear toughened plastic screen makes air flow up and over the rider at high speed.

HONDA

CBR

Brake pad presses on disc

Steel brake disc

Hydraulic fluid pushes a piston that presses the brake pad against the disc

Brake pipe

Disc rotates with wheel

✳ How do BRAKES work?

A disc brake has a large metal disc attached to the wheel. Brake pads made of very hard material, such as composite ceramic, press on this to cause friction and slow down the disc's rotation. The force to push the pads onto the disc may come from a cable attached to the brake lever. Or it can be hydraulic, from oil that is forced at high pressure from the brake lever or brake pedal along the brake pipe.

Streamline fairing

Brake disc

Radiator scoop This low opening collects air to flow over the radiator just behind it, which contains the water that keeps the engine cool.

HONI

Find out more about how brakes work by visiting
www.factsforprojects.com and clicking on the web link.

Since the Superbike World Championships began in 1988, makers Honda and Ducati have won all but two of the yearly titles.

Apart from being a nickname for a fast bike, 'Superbike' is also an official category of motorcycle racing for engines up to 1200cc.

✳ QUAD BIKES

A mix of car and motorcycle, quad bikes have four wheels but no main body or covering for the rider. A quad bike is difficult to handle because it tends to tip over if the rider steers around a corner too fast. It's great fun for riding over muddy fields and rough tracks.

Quad bikes have plenty of suspension

Exhaust

Swingarm The U-shaped swingarm tilts up and down at its joint with the frame so the rear wheel can move up and down as part of the suspension.

Tyres Racing superbikes have smooth or 'slick' tyres with no pattern or tread for good grip at high speed.

Three-spoked wheel

Water-cooled engine

Gear pedal Depending on which gear the motorcycle is already in, flipping the foot pedal up or down changes to the next gear.

Lightweight alloy wheels

15

SALOON CAR

The typical saloon car has been around for about 100 years and its basic design has hardly changed. It has four wheels, an engine in a compartment at the front that drives the front or rear wheels, two front seats and two or three rear seats in the main body. It also has a separate luggage compartment, or boot, at the rear.

Eureka!

The first petrol-engined automobile or 'car' (motorized carriage) was built by Karl Benz in 1885. It only had three wheels, the front one being steered by a lever.

Whatever next?

Cars of the future may drive themselves using GPS (satellite navigation) and radio links to a massive central computer.

Engine Typical family cars have engines from 2000cc (two litres) upwards. Usually there are four or six cylinders, one behind the other. The V8 shown here has two rows of four cylinders at a 'V' angle (see page 21).

Front suspension Upper and lower suspension arms allow the front wheels to move up and down.

How do PETROL ENGINES work?

A petrol engine has a piston that moves up and down inside a cylinder. It works in four stages, or strokes.

1. Inlet The piston moves down and sucks a mixture of fuel and air into the cylinder through an inlet valve.

2. Compression The piston moves up and squashes (compresses) the mixture.

3. Combustion An electric spark plug makes the mixture explode, forcing the piston down.

4. Exhaust The piston goes back up and pushes the burnt mixture out through an exhaust valve. The piston's movements turn the engine's crankshaft, by a con-rod.

Headlight

Radiator grill

In the early 20th century, the fastest cars were steam-powered or electric

Fuel mixture enters engine through inlet valve

Inlet valve closes and piston moves up, compressing fuel mixture

Exploding mixture forces piston down

Spark plug

Exhaust valve opens, burnt mixture leaves as exhaust gases

Cylinder

Piston

Con-rod

Con-rod turns crankshaft

Crankcase

Stroke 1

Crankshaft

Stroke 2

Stroke 3

Stroke 4

Watch an animation of the four-stroke engine in action by visiting www.factsforprojects.com and clicking on the web link.

ASTON MARTIN SALOON

In 1908 the mass-produced Ford Model T or 'Tin Lizzy' meant that ordinary people could afford a car.

Rear transmission The prop shaft is linked by the gears to the rear half-shaft axles on the wheels.

Propeller shaft Many saloon cars are front wheel drive. In the rear wheel drive design (shown here), the propeller shaft carries the turning power from the gearbox, along the underside of the car to the rear wheels.

Alloy wheels

The most successful car of all time is the Toyota Corolla, which began production in 1966. More than 35 million have been sold.

In the 1960s the tiny Austin Mini was a 'must-have' fashion car, with a transverse engine driving the front wheels to save space.

An all-electric car gets a kerbside charge

⁂ GREEN CARS

'Hybrid' cars have a small petrol engine and an electric motor with batteries. The car can run on electricity very quietly with no polluting exhaust fumes. If the batteries run down, the petrol engine switches on to recharge them. The petrol engine can also add power to the electric motor for more speed.

SUPER SPORTS CAR

For people with plenty of money, sports cars with powerful engines are the top road machines. They have little room for the week's shopping and would scrape along bumpy tracks, but they are sleek, speedy and striking. The low design and smooth lines allow the car to slip along with the least air resistance, which becomes more important as you travel faster.

Eureka!

The first wings appeared on sports cars and racing cars in the 1960s. They work like an upside-down aircraft wing to press the car downwards for better tyre grip and improved steering.

Whatever next?

Bugatti, maker of the world's leading supercar, the Veyron, plan a new model within five years to hold onto the sports car top spot.

The Bugatti Veyron was introduced in 2005 as the fastest production car in the world. It's also one of the most expensive, costing more than one million euros.

The Veyron is named after Pierre Veyron, the racing driver who won the 1939 Le Mans 24 Hour race in a Bugatti.

Retractable wing The rear wing is known as a spoiler. If you want to travel at speeds of between 200 and 370 kilometres per hour in the Veyron, a switch lowers the car and wing, which then disturbs air flow that might suck the car upwards.

W16 engine The W16 engine is a double version of the V8 engine, with 16 cylinders in four rows of four at an angle, like two overlapping Vs.

How does a GEARBOX work?

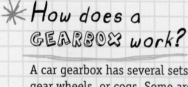

A car gearbox has several sets of spinning gear wheels, or cogs. Some are on the layshaft, an 'extra' shaft between the drive shaft from the engine and the shaft to the road wheels. The gear change mechanism works by sliding the gear collar along a shaft so that it rotates to make the cogs fit together in different combinations. This makes the road wheels turn faster or slower for the same engine speed.

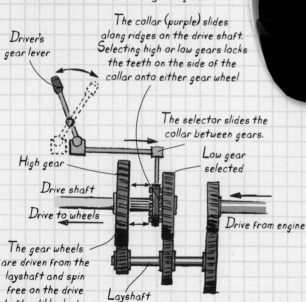

Driver's gear lever

The collar (purple) slides along ridges on the drive shaft. Selecting high or low gears locks the teeth on the side of the collar onto either gear wheel

The selector slides the collar between gears.

High gear

Low gear selected

Drive shaft

Drive to wheels

Drive from engine

The gear wheels are driven from the layshaft and spin free on the drive shaft until locked on by the collar

Layshaft

Exhaust pipe

Gearbox The seven-speed gearbox is computer controlled and can change gear in less than one-fifth of a second. The driver uses small gear-shift paddles next to the steering wheel.

To learn more about gear boxes visit
www.factsforprojects.com and click on the web link.

The Bugatti Veyron has a total of ten radiators, including three for the engine and two for the air conditioning!

Le Mans drivers practise for weeks

✳ LE MANS 24 HOUR

One of the world's most famous races, the Le Mans race for sports cars lasts 24 hours non-stop. Only one car is allowed per team, but three drivers can take turns, although none can stay at the wheel for more than four hours at a time. The cars come into the pits 30-plus times and cover more than 5000 kilometres at average speeds above 200 kilometres per hour.

Brakes The brake discs are carbon composite and the pistons that push on them are titanium metal, so they are less affected by great heat.

BUGATTI VEYRON

Bugatti have made many amazing cars over the years. The massive Royale of the 1920s had a 12-litre engine and a bonnet longer than many modern small cars.

Propeller shaft In a mid- or rear-engined four-wheel-drive sports car, the prop shaft carries the engine's turning power to the front wheels.

Half-shaft Each road wheel has its own short axle, or half-shaft. The Veyron is a four-wheel drive vehicle.

Wide low-profile tyres

Alloy wheels

19

F1 RACING CAR

Formula One cars are not the biggest racing machines, or the fastest, or the most powerful. But for all-round performance on a twisty track, speeding up and then braking hard to scream around corners, they cannot be beaten. An F1 car is built according to more than 1000 rules and regulations, from engine size to overall weight, the electronic sensors it must have, and using the same gearbox for four races in a row.

Eureka!

After many kinds of races with different cars and rules, the first F1 season was in 1950. There are about 18 races around the world in a year. Each race is more than 300 kilometres long but lasts less than two hours.

Whatever next?

The Rocket Racing League plans to hold races for rocket-powered cars and aircraft, each lasting between 60 and 90 minutes.

Telemetry Sensors for speed, brake temperature and many other features send information by radio signals to the team members in the pits.

Suspension arm The suspension arms swing to allow the wheel to move up and down.

Mirrors

Front wing The front wing produces about one-third of the down force of the rear wing. It keeps the front tyres pressed hard onto the track for accurate steering. The upright end plates direct air smoothly over the wheels.

An F1's engine is part of the car's structure, bolted to the driver's cockpit at the front, and the transmission and rear suspension at the back.

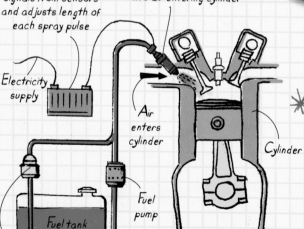

Nose cone

ECU (electronic control unit) receives signals from sensors and adjusts length of each spray pulse

Fuel injector squirts fuel into air entering cylinder

Electricity supply

Air enters cylinder

Cylinder

Fuel pump

Fuel tank

Fuel pressure regulator allows unused fuel back to the tank

✳ How does FUEL INJECTION work?

A fuel injector squirts fuel, under pressure from a fuel pump, into air being sucked into the cylinder. An electronic control unit calculates how much fuel per squirt, depending on sensor information such as air pressure, engine speed and how much oxygen is in the exhaust gases (which is linked to how much fuel is left unburnt).

Tyres There are tyres for dry conditions, wet conditions and intermediate (in between). Dry tyres are slicks with no tread pattern.

Watch amazing videos of Formula One races by visiting www.factsforprojects.com and clicking on the web link.

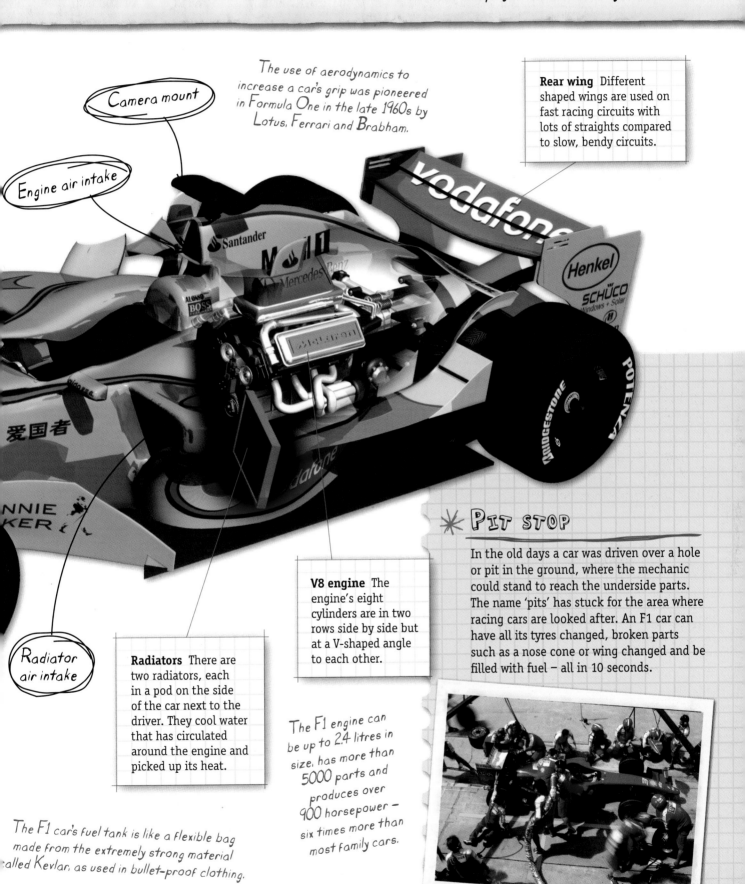

Camera mount

Engine air intake

The use of aerodynamics to increase a car's grip was pioneered in Formula One in the late 1960s by Lotus, Ferrari and Brabham.

Rear wing Different shaped wings are used on fast racing circuits with lots of straights compared to slow, bendy circuits.

Radiator air intake

Radiators There are two radiators, each in a pod on the side of the car next to the driver. They cool water that has circulated around the engine and picked up its heat.

V8 engine The engine's eight cylinders are in two rows side by side but at a V-shaped angle to each other.

The F1 engine can be up to 2.4 litres in size, has more than 5000 parts and produces over 900 horsepower – six times more than most family cars.

The F1 car's fuel tank is like a flexible bag made from the extremely strong material called Kevlar, as used in bullet-proof clothing.

✳ PIT STOP

In the old days a car was driven over a hole or pit in the ground, where the mechanic could stand to reach the underside parts. The name 'pits' has stuck for the area where racing cars are looked after. An F1 car can have all its tyres changed, broken parts such as a nose cone or wing changed and be filled with fuel – all in 10 seconds.

The Ferrari pit crew work quickly to prepare the car

DRAGSTER

Dragster racing is the world's loudest, fastest form of motor racing – yet each race has only two competitors, no corners and lasts just a few seconds. The idea is to accelerate (pick up speed) as quickly as possible from a standing start, to be first across the finish line 402.3 metres (one-quarter of a mile) or 201 metres (one-eighth of a mile) away.

Eureka!

In 1951, Wally Parks had the idea of making unofficial and dangerous dragster-type street racing into an official sport. He founded the US National Hot Rod Association, which has run the sport since.

Whatever next?

Some drivers have experimented with jump ramps halfway along the drag strip (track) so that the race is half on the ground and half flying through the air!

Dragsters have just one gear – there's no time to change to a second one.

Streamlined body The lightweight body is long, slim and tapering so that it slices through the air like an arrow.

Cockpit

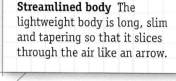

Twin 'meshing' impellers suck in and compress the air

Impellers spin around

Air blasted into carburettor

Roller bearing

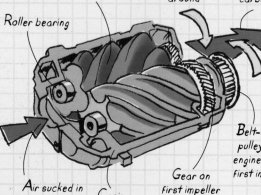

Air sucked in   Casing   Gear on first impeller drives second impeller

Belt-driven pulley from engine drives first impeller

✳ How does a SUPERCHARGER work?

A supercharger forces air into the engine at high pressure so it carries extra fuel for greater speed and power. It consists of two screw-like devices called impellers that suck in air through an inlet and blast it from the outlet into the carburettor. The impellers are driven by a belt or chain from the engine. Turbochargers are similar but use a fan-like turbine rather than a direct mechanical drive (see page 28).

Front wheels The tiny front wheels mean less weight and air resistance. The front wing keeps them pushed onto the track.

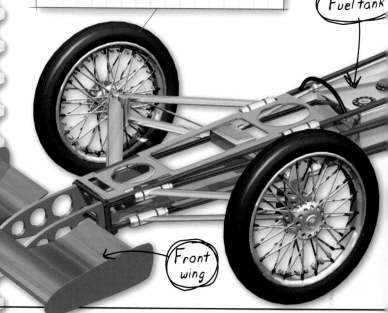

Fuel tank

Front wing

See drag racing in action by visiting
www.factsforprojects.com and clicking on the web link.

The huge rear
tyres on top-fuel
dragsters wear out
after about five
races – less than
2 km. Ordinary car
tyres usually last
30,000 km or more.

Smoke at the 'burnout'

✳ WHACKY RACERS!

There are dozens of types or classes of
dragster racing, depending on engine
size and type of fuel. Before the start
the enormous rear tyres are spun against
the ground in a 'burnout' while the
dragster stays still, to make them hot
and sticky so they grip better.

Roll cage Drivers
sit within a tubular
metal frame or
cage that gives
protection if the
dragster rolls over.

The fastest dragsters cross the finish line at more than 530 km/h –
almost five times the British motorway speed limit.

Air intake
manifold

Rear wing

Instrument panel

Supercharger

Short stub
exhausts

Rear wheels The huge
rear wheels have soft,
slick (treadless) tyres.
The driver and engine
are both near the back
so that their weight
helps the tyres to press
down and grip.

Tubular alloy chassis
The light but stiff
chassis (the main
framework) is made
of various alloys or
mixtures of metals.

Top-fuel dragsters,
the fastest type, use
about 20 litres of fuel
during the race, which
is about 800 times
more than a family car
would use.

Supercharged V8 engine
The largest engine in
most races is 8.2 litres.
Its supercharger means
it can produce over 5000
horsepower.

4WD OFF-ROADER

A four-wheeled vehicle with four-wheel drive (4WD or 4x4) means that all four wheels are turned by engine power. A 4x2 vehicle has four wheels but only two are engine-powered, while 6x4 is a six-wheeled vehicle with engine power to four wheels. Four-wheel drive is best for ATVs – All-Terrain Vehicles that can go off-road and across almost any kind of terrain or ground, from soft sand to squashy mud to steep rocky slopes.

Eureka!

Car designers who built the first 4WD vehicles in the 1900s included Ferdinand Porsche, founder of the famous Porsche sports car and racing car organization. His first 4WD had an electric motor for each wheel. On some types of 4WDs all the four wheels steer, not just two.

Whatever next?

Military off-road vehicles have tested 4WDs with an extra two wheels that swing down to give added grip in the slippiest mud.

EXPLODED VIEW OF HUMVEE

The Humvee's engine air intake, exhaust, electrical wires and similar parts are designed so that the vehicle can drive through water more than one metre deep.

Snorkel Air for the engine is sucked in through a tall pipe to avoid taking in water while crossing streams.

Camouflage Military vehicles such as the Humvee are painted so they blend in with their surroundings. This is called camouflage.

The military 4WD called the Humvee is used by US and other military forces around the world.

Lights

Tow points

Radiator The radiator is well protected against damage from rocks by a strong metal plate underneath.

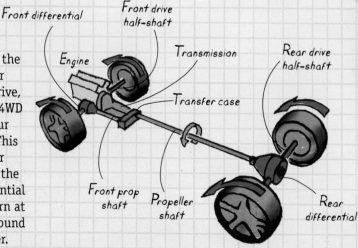

✳ How does 4WD work?

In some cars a front engine drives the two rear wheels by a long propeller shaft. Most cars are front-wheel drive, with half-shafts at the front. The 4WD system combines the two so all four wheels turn under engine power. This gives much better grip on rough or slippery surfaces, especially when the tyres have a deep tread. The differential makes the two wheels it powers turn at different speeds, so when going around a corner, the outer one turns faster.

Front differential

Engine

Front drive half-shaft

Transmission

Rear drive half-shaft

Transfer case

Front prop shaft

Propeller shaft

Rear differential

Humvees are so tough they can be dropped by parachute from cargo planes.

Discover everything there is to know about the Humvee by
visiting www.factsforprojects.com and clicking on the web link.

Machine gun The rotating roof turret, or cupola, with its armoured guard, can be fitted with a powerful machine gun.

Armour plating Thick, strong but light metal plates cover most of the bodywork to protect against bullets, land mines and other dangers.

The Humvee is named from its initials, HMMWV, meaning High Mobility Multi-purpose Wheeled Vehicle.

High exhaust

The Hummer can tackle any kind of difficult terrain

Engine Military 4WDs such as the Humvee have a 6.5 litre diesel engine with fuel injection.

Chassis The main frame has two long girder-like rails and several cross-members.

✳ MUSCLE-MACHINE!

The Humvee 4WD is available as a civilian (non-military) version – the Hummer 1. There are many other types of 4WDs used by farmers, foresters, ranchers, explorers, countryside workers and of course drivers keen on off-roading. Movie star and US politician Arnold Schwarzenegger has a 'green' Hummer that's been converted to run on non-polluting hydrogen fuel.

RALLY CAR

Rallies are tough races that can take place almost anywhere, from public roads (closed to everyday traffic for the event) to dirt tracks, forest trails, ice and snow, deserts and real racing circuits. A rally car is a special version of a normal production car that has a tuned-up engine and stronger mechanical parts.

The Dakar Rally is the longest, hardest race. It runs more than 10,000 km from European cities to Dakar, Senegal, in West Africa. Part of the race is across the Sahara Desert.

Eureka!

Before satnav (satellite navigation), which uses GPS (the Global Positioning System of satellites), rally drivers sometimes got lost and ended up dozens of kilometres from the finish line.

Tough suspension The springs, shock absorber dampers and other suspension parts take a huge hammering on rallies.

✳ ON THE SPEEDWAY

Stock cars are ordinary production cars with certain changes and modifications, as allowed by the rules, to compete on proper racing circuits. In the USA they roar around giant oval tracks called speedways as part of the NASCAR season – the National Association for Stock Car Auto Racing. NASCAR drivers can reach speeds of more than 300 kilometres per hour.

Stock cars on the NASCAR 'bowl'

Rear differential The 'diff' can be 'locked' to make both rear wheels turn at the same speed for getting out of holes and ditches.

Lowered body

Rally cars are 4WD and based on 2-litre turbocharged engines.

Brakes Heavy duty brakes mean that rally drivers can brake at the last split second as they enter corners to clock up the fastest time.

Whatever next?

Inventors have built 'amphibious' cars that have wheels for normal road conditions, plus floats with propellers to travel through water like a boat.

Learn about different types of steering systems by visiting www.factsfor projects.com and clicking on the web link.

Roll cage A framework of strong tubes inside the passenger compartment stops the sides or roof caving in if there's a crash.

The World Rally Championship consists of about 15 or 16 races all around the world.

Internal padding All hard objects near the driver and co-driver are padded to avoid injury when bouncing along rough roads.

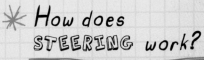

Steering wheel

Steering shaft

Track rod

Pinion

Rack

Front wheel

Turning the steering wheel causes the rack to move left or right

Steering arm

Steering rack and pinion

✳ How does STEERING work?

A car's steering wheel is fixed to a long shaft called a steering column, with a small gear called a pinion at its base. As the pinion turns it makes a rack – a long bar with teeth – slide left or right. Each end of the rack is linked to a smaller bar known as a track rod, which is attached by a ball joint to another bar, the steering arm, and this is attached to each front wheel hub. As the rack slides left or right, it moves the track rod and steering arm. The steering arm works as a lever to make the front wheels angle left or right.

Tuned transverse engine The engine is carefully adjusted, or tuned, so that it runs with the greatest power yet does not use too much fuel. This saves fuel weight and also reduces the number of refuelling stops.

Alternator (generator)

Spotlights

PICK-UP TRUCK

If you want to transport a heavy load, a pick-up truck is the ideal vehicle. These small but tough trucks have an open flat area called a load bed for their cargo. Some are two- or three-seaters with one row of seats, others have a second row behind the driver. The strengthened, stiffened rear suspension means the ride is not as comfortable as an ordinary car.

Pick-up racing is a fast and furious motor sport where the modified trucks can speed along at more than 200 km/h.

Eureka!

In the early years of motoring, people cut the rear body off a car and added a wooden platform to make a pick-up truck. The first mass-produced versions based on the Ford Model T were sold in 1925.

Whatever next?

Some pick-ups have a container that folds out and opens up to become a caravan-style living place or mobile home.

One travelling circus in the USA had an elephant specially trained to ride on the back of a pick-up truck.

Engine Most pick-ups have diesel engines. These are heavy and noisy but powerful and easy to adjust and maintain.

Tinted glass

✳ How does a TURBODIESEL work?

A diesel engine is similar to a petrol engine (see page 16) but it lacks spark plugs. The air-fuel mixture explodes in the cylinder because it gets hot from being squeezed so much. The turbocharger, or 'turbo', is similar to a supercharger (see page 22) but the impeller that forces extra air into the engine is worked by a fan-like turbine spun around by exhaust gases.

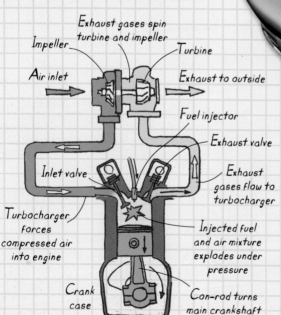

Impeller
Exhaust gases spin turbine and impeller
Turbine
Air inlet
Exhaust to outside
Fuel injector
Exhaust valve
Inlet valve
Exhaust gases flow to turbocharger
Turbocharger forces compressed air into engine
Injected fuel and air mixture explodes under pressure
Crank case
Con-rod turns main crankshaft

Foglights

Tyres Pick-ups have thick, wide, strong tyres to spread the weight, and knobbly tread to grip soft ground.

In Australia, pick-up trucks are often called 'utes' (utility vehicles).

Turb

To learn about modified pick-up trucks with monster wheels
visit www.factsforprojects.com and click on the web link.

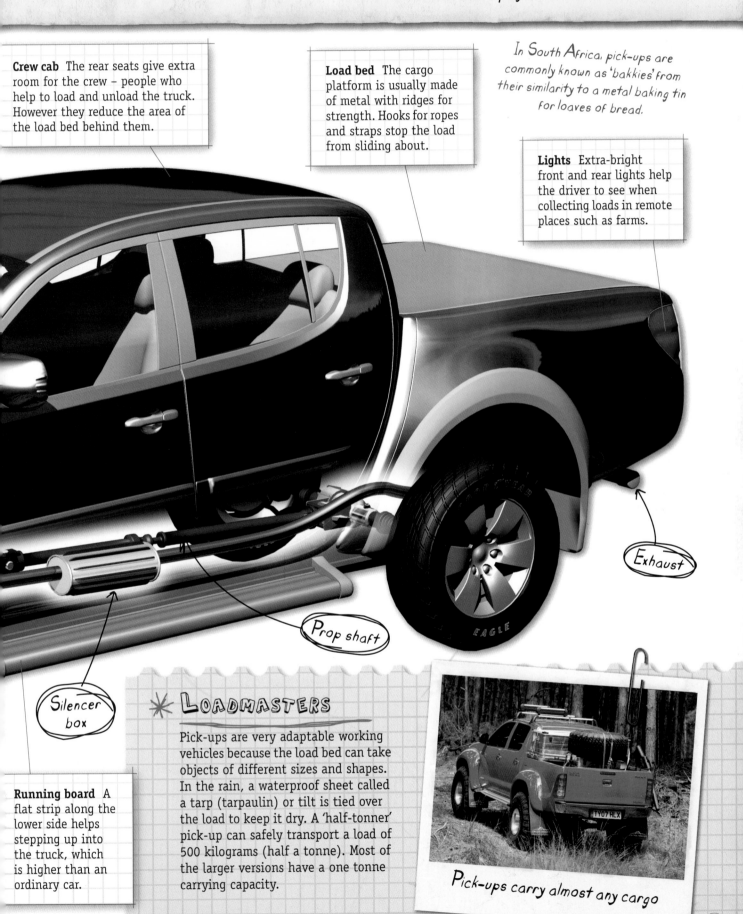

Crew cab The rear seats give extra room for the crew – people who help to load and unload the truck. However they reduce the area of the load bed behind them.

Load bed The cargo platform is usually made of metal with ridges for strength. Hooks for ropes and straps stop the load from sliding about.

In South Africa, pick-ups are commonly known as 'bakkies' from their similarity to a metal baking tin for loaves of bread.

Lights Extra-bright front and rear lights help the driver to see when collecting loads in remote places such as farms.

Exhaust

Prop shaft

Silencer box

Running board A flat strip along the lower side helps stepping up into the truck, which is higher than an ordinary car.

✳ LOADMASTERS

Pick-ups are very adaptable working vehicles because the load bed can take objects of different sizes and shapes. In the rain, a waterproof sheet called a tarp (tarpaulin) or tilt is tied over the load to keep it dry. A 'half-tonner' pick-up can safely transport a load of 500 kilograms (half a tonne). Most of the larger versions have a one tonne carrying capacity.

Pick-ups carry almost any cargo

CITY BUS

There are many kinds of passenger-carrying buses and coaches for different services. Some carry fewer people long distances in comfort, with soft seats and lots of legroom. Others pack in as many people as possible, often standing up, for short trips around towns and cities. In some places electric buses are replacing diesel-engined ones, to keep city streets quieter and the air cleaner.

Eureka!

The earliest 'buses' in the 1700s were horse-drawn wagons with two benches along the middle. The passengers sat back-to-back, facing sideways. There were no sides or roof to keep out the wind and rain.

Whatever next?

The latest long-distance buses have screens for computers or movies and earphones for music, like a long-haul passenger aircraft.

Automatic doors
The driver works buttons that make the passenger door swing open using an electric mechanism.

One of the world's biggest buses is the Superliner from Shanghai, China. At 25 m long it can carry up to 300 passengers and bend to go around corners.

Rack and pinion steering

An articulated bus in London

✳ BENDY BUSES

Many old cities have narrow streets and sharp corners unsuitable for long buses. The articulated (jointed) or 'bendy' bus, has a link in the middle so it can turn corners more tightly than a rigid one-piece vehicle. Some bendy buses have two links joining three sections. The driver keeps watch on the rear end using closed-circuit television cameras and a screen – CCTV.

Driver-only Most modern buses are driver-only. The driver collects the money and gives out tickets. Some buses have a driver and a conductor, who collects the fare.

Read facts and view pictures of many different kinds of buses by visiting www.factsforprojects.com and clicking on the web link.

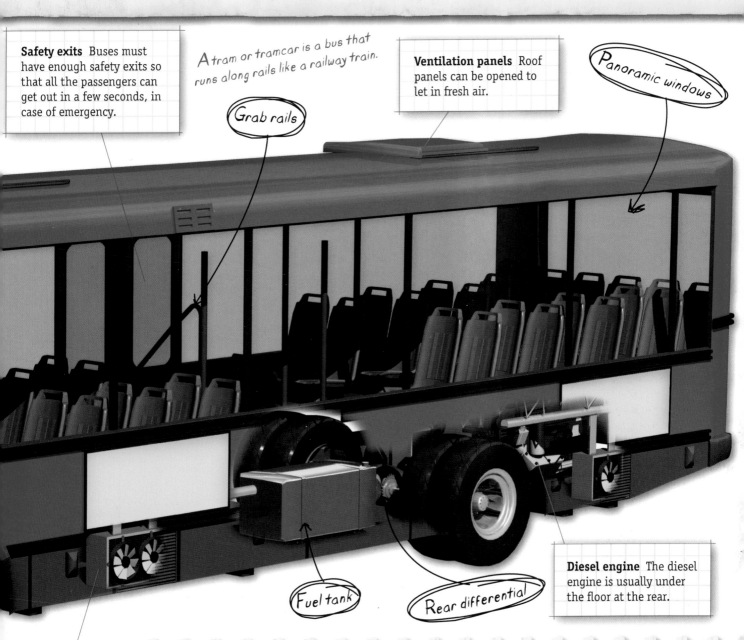

Safety exits Buses must have enough safety exits so that all the passengers can get out in a few seconds, in case of emergency.

A tram or tramcar is a bus that runs along rails like a railway train.

Grab rails

Ventilation panels Roof panels can be opened to let in fresh air.

Panoramic windows

Fuel tank

Rear differential

Diesel engine The diesel engine is usually under the floor at the rear.

Air conditioning The air inside the bus is heated or cooled depending on the outside temperature.

A trolley bus is an electric bus that gets its electricity from long 'arms' that touch overhead wires.

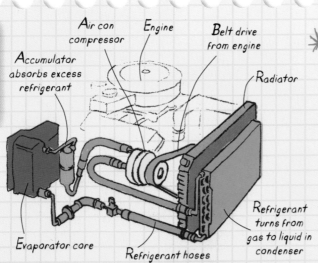

Air con compressor

Engine

Belt drive from engine

Accumulator absorbs excess refrigerant

Radiator

Evaporator core

Refrigerant hoses

Refrigerant turns from gas to liquid in condenser

✳ How does **AIR CON** work?

Air conditioning, or climate control, works in a similar way to a fridge. A compressor squeezes a gas, the refrigerant, flowing around a circuit of pipes. The compressed gas condenses and becomes a liquid and in the process gets hot. In the second part of the circuit the pressure is lower, so the liquid refrigerant expands and evaporates (turns back into a gas) and in the process becomes much colder.

ARTICULATED TRUCK

The 'artic' is a truck that is articulated, or jointed. The joint is between the front part – the tractor unit with the engine and driver's cab – and the rear part, or trailer, which carries the load. The joint allows the truck to go around tighter corners than a one-piece vehicle. It also means different kinds of trailers can be joined, or hitched, to the tractor unit.

Eureka!

The first artics were built in the 1910s by Charles Martin. He hitched a tractor-like truck to a wagon usually pulled by horses. Martin also invented the fifth wheel coupling between tractor unit and trailer (below).

Whatever next?

Most countries limit the size of trucks by their weight or length. However new super-highways could see trucks of 100 tonnes or more.

Trailer

The ShockWave truck of Hawaii's Fire Department has two jet engines and can reach speeds of 600 km/h. It's only used for shows, not to race to real fires.

Fifth wheel is well greased to reduce friction

Rear of cab

Trailer's king pin engages in slot

✴ How does the FIFTH WHEEL work?

The 'fifth wheel coupling' is the joint or link between the tractor unit and trailer. It consists of a king pin or coupling pin on the lower front of the trailer that slides up on and then slots into the U-shaped fifth wheel on the rear of the tractor unit. The trailer can swing from side to side behind the tractor unit and also move by a small amount up or down to cope with bumpy roads.

Trailer stands
When the trailer is unhitched its front leans on these strong metal legs.

The Centipede truck is 55 m long and weighs 205 tonnes – the longest truck in regular work.

Find out everything there is to know about ice road truckers by visiting
www.factsforprojects.com and clicking on the web link.

A road train is one tractor unit pulling several trailers, like a railway locomotive pulls several carriages. Some road trains are more than 1000 m long and weigh 1000-plus tonnes.

Roof fairing Even on a 40-tonne truck, smooth streamlining helps to lower air resistance. This increases speed and reduces fuel use.

In the USA, artics are called semi-trailer trucks, and the tractor unit is the towing engine.

Cab controls A big truck has ten gears for all conditions, from cruising the open road with no load to climbing a steep hill with 30-plus tonnes of cargo on the back.

Tractor unit

Sun visor

Fifth wheel

VOLVO

520

Engine Truck turbodiesel engines are 11, 13 or 16 litres, sometimes even more.

King pin

Fuel tank A family car's fuel tank holds around 70 litres. A big artic carries 500 litres, and sometimes over 2000 litres.

✳ ICE ROAD TRUCKERS

Sometimes it's quicker for a car or truck to get to a remote place across a lake – provided it's frozen. Ice truckers specialize in carrying loads across the far north in winter, to faraway places such as mining centres and logging camps. The truckers keep in radio contact with each other about snowdrifts, cracks or melting ice.

An artic heads across a frozen lake

BREAKDOWN TRUCK

Everyone on the road fears a sudden breakdown. Soon after mass motoring began in the 1900s, specialized trucks were rescuing stranded drivers and recovering their broken vehicles. It's important to clear the road and get the vehicle out of danger, then take it to a suitable garage for repair. This may have to be done at night, in heavy rain or in thick fog or snow. Breakdown, recovery or tow trucks are strong, tough and able to cope with all conditions.

Eureka!

Mechanic Ernest Holmes built the first breakdown truck in 1915. He fixed three metal poles, a chain and a pulley to a 1913 Cadillac in Chattanooga, Tennessee, USA, and began the tow truck business.

Whatever next?

Motoring experts are working on 'intelligent' vehicle electronics to sense which part has broken and then radio the breakdown truck to bring it as soon as possible.

Powerful engine The turbodiesel engine must be powerful enough to move two vehicles, perhaps across soft ground if the broken-down one has veered off the road.

✳ How does a WINCH work?

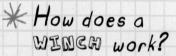

A winch has a strong metal cable or wire that winds slowly onto a drum. Some breakdown truck winches are electric with a powerful motor worked by the truck's battery. Others are driven by the truck's engine. The turning speed is greatly reduced by gear cogs, so that as the turning speed goes down, the turning force or torque goes up. The cable winds very slowly but with huge force to drag or lift the broken-down vehicle.

The world's biggest breakdown trucks are converted Caterpillar 793s, used in mines to recover giant haulage trucks weighing over 400 tonnes.

Visor

Air filter

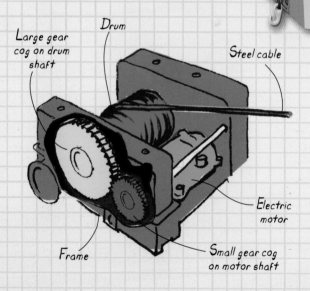

Large gear cog on drum shaft

Drum

Steel cable

Frame

Electric motor

Small gear cog on motor shaft

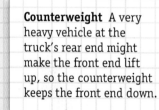

Counterweight A very heavy vehicle at the truck's rear end might make the front end lift up, so the counterweight keeps the front end down.

The International Towing and Recovery Hall of Fame and Museum are in Chattanooga, USA, near where Ernest Holmes started the first breakdown truck business.

The AA, Automobile Association, started in 1905. Its patrol staff were equipped with two-way radios in the late 1940s. Before that, they phoned HQ regularly to find out if there were any breakdowns nearby.

Read about the history of vehicle recovery by visiting
www.factsforprojects.com and clicking on the web link.

Flashing lights

Winch The steel cable from the hoist hook winds slowly onto the winch drum.

Boom The boom (lift-arm or crane) is worked by two powerful hydraulic jacks. Its L-shaped end can be slotted underneath the front of a vehicle to raise it from beneath, instead of using the hook.

Britain's first motoring organization was the RAC (Royal Automobile Club), formed in 1897 for breakdown help. It introduced roadside emergency telephone boxes in 1912.

Hook

Ramps The rear ramps can be lowered to support the broken vehicle's front wheels.

Eight rear wheels spread load

Step

Tools A large tool compartment contains spanners, crowbars, screwdrivers, cutters and other essential equipment.

A flatbed (rollback or slide) truck recovers a broken-down car

✳ SLIDING UP AND ON

There are several kinds of breakdown or tow trucks. Some have crane-like booms to lift vehicles straight up out of ditches or rivers. Some have an arm and winch to drag the broken vehicle to safety. Others have a flat rear platform or flatbed that slides backwards and down onto the road, so the vehicle can be winched onto it. Then the platform slides back up.

FIRE ENGINE

Firefighting appliances, or trucks, (fire engines) may be first to arrive at big incidents – and not just fires, but floods, road accidents, people trapped down holes or in high places and even kittens in trees. The appliance sprays water or special types of chemical foam depending on the type of fire and what is burning, such as wood, plastic or fuels.

Eureka!

The first firefighting wagons were hauled by people, or horses, or both. Self-propelled appliances powered by steam engines were used in New York from 1841 and in London and other British cities from the 1850s.

Whatever next?

Fire crews carry out regular tests on new siren noises – although they warn people they are nearby – one sounds like a whining dog!

Flashing lights

Siren The siren is worked by an electric motor and fan that pumps air past a specially shaped hole into a tube, similar to blowing a trumpet.

✳ EXTENDING LADDERS

Multi-section ladders extend like a telescope mounted on a turntable on the fire vehicle. They can reach up to 30 metres – the 10th floor of a high-rise building. The crew member at the upper end of the ladder is in radio contact with the ladder operator below so that the ladder can be put into exactly the correct position. Spraying water or foam onto a fire from above is far more effective than from the side.

The extending ladder gets above the fire

Fire and ambulance crews refer to a call-out for an emergency as a 'shout'.

Engine The diesel engine is started regularly to make sure it works when needed.

Take an on-line tour of a fire engine by visiting
www.factsforprojects.com and clicking on the web link.

Hoses One set of hoses connects to a nearby water supply to draw water in. Another set carries the water away to spray on the fire. The hoses wind onto reels turned by electric motors.

Mains supply pipes

Screw fittings link pipes

✳ How do HYDRAULICS work?

Hydraulic machinery, such as a fire appliance's cutters or extending ladder, works using high-pressure liquid (water or oil). Like a lever, the liquid changes a small force moving a long distance into a big force moving a short distance. The small force presses on a narrow piston to create pressure throughout the fluid. This pushes a wider piston with greater force because of its larger surface area.

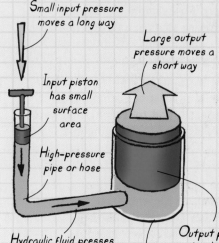

Small input pressure moves a long way

Large output pressure moves a short way

Input piston has small surface area

High-pressure pipe or hose

Hydraulic fluid presses in all directions with equal pressure

Cylinder

Output piston has large surface area

Wheel hub

London's Fire Brigade has more than 250 appliances including 30 aerial ladder platforms.

Control panel The switches and other controls are for the main pumps that force water or foam along the hose, showing its pressure and flow rate.

Some fire appliances have pumps so powerful they can spray a distance of more than 70 m.

Tools The standard appliance carries a host of useful tools including powerful hydraulic cutters and spreaders worked by high-pressure hoses from the diesel engine.

EXPLODED VIEW

INDEX